Dating While Waiting

Staying True to Your Purity Vow

SYDRA L. WESTON

DATING WHILE WAITING
STAYING TRUE TO YOUR PURITY VOW

Holy Bible, New Living Translation, copyright © 1996, 2004, 2015 by Tyndale House Foundation. Used by permission of Tyndale House Publishers Inc., Carol Stream, Illinois 60188. All rights reserved.

The Holy Bible, New International Version®, NIV® Copyright © 1973, 1978, 1984, 2011 by Biblica, Inc.® Used by permission. All rights reserved worldwide.

Scripture taken from The Message. Copyright © 1993, 1994, 1995, 1996, 2000, 2001, 2002. Used by permission of NavPress Publishing Group.

The Authorized (King James) Version of the Bible ("the KJV"), the rights in which are vested in the Crown in the United Kingdom, is reproduced here by permission of the Crown's patentee, Cambridge University Press.

The Cambridge KJV text, including paragraphing, is reproduced here by permission of Cambridge University Press.

iUniverse books may be ordered through booksellers or by contacting:

iUniverse
1663 Liberty Drive
Bloomington, IN 47403
www.iuniverse.com
1-800-Authors (1-800-288-4677)

ISBN: 978-1-5320-2207-4 (sc)
ISBN: 978-1-5320-2208-1 (e)

Library of Congress Control Number: 2017907139

Print information available on the last page.

iUniverse rev. date: 06/20/2017

A gift for

_____

From

_____

On this date

_____

This book is dedicated to:

Earnestine Freeman (Grandma) and Mattie Douglas (Mommy) thank you for praying for me, with me—, and for showing me how to pray. Thank you both for introducing me to Jesus Christ at a young age and for praying for my salvation. You both have shown me that a family that prays together truly stays together.

Thank you, Kelsey M. Cade, for being such an inspiration for this book. I want to be the big cousin to you that I always wanted in my life. Thanks for being so open and letting me pick your teenage brain. P.S. Here's your 10 percent. Love you, Mimi!

Contents

Acknowledgments

First and foremost, if it hadn't been for the Lord who is on my side, where would I be? For that, Lord, I give you all the praise. I thank you for saving me at the age of thirteen—even when I didn't fully understand all that it entailed. All thanks and praise belongs to you.

To my brothers, Nicholas and Brian, thank you for being supportive of me and my dreams. You both are such a blessing to me. In the words of Brian, "We know how to have oodles of fun with each other."

To my sister, Alexa, ever since I could remember, I always wanted a sister—and God blessed me to be a big sister to you. I know there's such a big age gap between us, but just know as you grow that I am here. You can talk to me about anything. I love you!

To my sissy and my friend, Marissa L. Lewis. You tell the truth even when I hate to hear your long lectures. Thank you for keeping it real, putting up with my sassy ways, and accepting all of me. I get on your last nerve—and you get on mine—but it works. Thank you. I love you!

To Billy Weston (Dad) and Donald Douglas/Mr. Q (Stepdad), you both have taught me the dos and don'ts of how a man should treat me, honor me, and protect me. You both have told me time and time again not to settle. You have provided for me, showed me how to be a lady, and taught me how a lady should be treated. I am truly grateful for the both of you. Thank you both for your covering.

Jayla Williams, thank you for being a part of the initial forum and for being open to allowing me to test my exercises with you and Kelsey.

To Pastor Edwards and Minister Norm, thank you for your prayers and blessings. Minister Norm, thank you for taking the time to review my manuscript and for offering me feedback that helped me dig deeper into the topics.

To Shirley Futch (mom), you didn't have to do it, but you did. You read the first draft of my manuscript and offered your feedback. You encouraged me to keep going. Love you and thank you!

Last—but definitely not least—thank you to my all my family and friends. Your support through the years has been such a blessing. To my roots (you know who you are), you have rocked with me from day one. I am truly grateful for each and every one of you. I am glad you allowed me to be myself without judgment. You have helped me learn and grow. You have wiped my tears at times, and I am blessed to have you in my life. Thank you, everyone!

Preface

Greetings! I am truly excited to be embarking on this journey with you. This book is written because, deep in my heart and soul, I've been craving to share the knowledge that I have learned over the years when it comes to being a Christian girl and dating. As I took a step back and allowed God into my dating life, he opened my eyes to how I was using the world's dating system instead of seeking his guidance in choosing a godly mate through him who would honor me and my purity.

As a mentor to girls, I have watched and observed them making the same mistakes I made. I recall after a breakup praying, crying, and talking to God, and telling him I was tired. I told him I was sorry for not trusting him and that I wished I had something that I could go to or someone I could talk to in the church to assist me with the struggles I was facing as a Christian girl who was trying to learn how to date through him.

I earned my master's degree in marketing management and began to research dating books that relate to Christianity. I ran some focus groups on the most popular topics, let some girls do the assessments in this book, and found out which topics worked and which didn't. I went to bookstores and libraries to find out what books were out there in relation to dating as a Christian girl and maintaining our purity.

I remember going into a bookstore and asking an employee—who looked to be about seventeen—where the purity books were.

She said, "What is that?"

I knew then that God was calling me to minister to girls through my experiences.

I invite every church, every library, and every home. Engage with your parents, friends, and teachers. Take notes and highlight things that jump out at you. Most importantly, I want you to have fun as we begin this journey of dating together—with God as the center of the process.

"WHATEVER I AM NOW, IT IS ALL BECAUSE GOD
POURED OUT HIS SPECIAL FAVOR ON ME."
—*1 Corinthians 15:10 (NLT)*

Introduction

Developing a Good Foundation

I grew up in a southern holiness church, and for as long as I can remember, people said, "No fornicating, no sex before marriage, no boys, no dating until you get out of my house and you are grown and living on your own, no kissing, no hugging, no, no, no." Nobody ever told me why.

I thought about fixing my lips and asking, "Why?"

I could hear the answer ringing ever so clearly: "Because I said so."

Like an inquisitive young lady who likes to push the envelope just a tad bit further, I asked, "Why?"

"This is my house and my rules."

"A lady is supposed to be seen and not heard."

"It's in the Bible"

Sometimes. Ephesians 6:1–3 was quoted to me.

I asked why so much that they had us study and memorize Ephesians 6:1–3 in Sunday school. No one would ever explain the why behind the no. If someone had taught me the why, I believe some situations I have encountered in my life could have been avoided. I would have been more aware of what I needed to be cautious of, I would have appreciated the word *no* with dating at my age, and I would have understood why my parents were so protective over me and my purity.

This brings me to why I was prompted to write this

book. This is for the young ladies—like myself at the time—who need to know the why to better understand the meaning of staying pure until God blesses you with a godly mate (your husband). This is for the preteens who are battling with themselves about how to keep holy and still be able to hang out with the in crowd. This book is for young adults who have experienced dating and are still trying to find themselves among the noise while keeping God in the forefront. Lastly, this book is for the single Christian young women who are continuing to keep God in the center—those who want to date while trying to keep it holy. This is for the young women who are battling with the changing times—and the times sure have changed since our parents and grandparents were dating, courting, and waiting for God to send their Boaz to find them.

I can't speak for everyone else, but I can speak for myself when I say that, throughout my spiritual teaching and growing up in church, no one dared to teach about dating as a Christian in the church. They never taught how to date as a Christian woman in the church, what feelings you may experience while dating, the pressures you may feel while dating, how to handle breakups, and all things relating to trials and tribulations you may encounter while waiting on a helpmeet.

Dating is an unspoken topic in church. It is taboo to talk about it in church. No one dares to tell the truth out of fear of being judged instead of looking at it as a way to help those who have struggled or are struggling to keep holy while trying to find themselves and the mate God has for them.

With this book, my goal is to open a platform for the church to train our kids in the way they should go and give guidance so that it's not sought elsewhere. Our youth may be confused by what they see on the television, what they read in magazines or on the Internet, or what they see in everyday interactions and observations.

God has spoken to my heart, and he has placed this burning message into my heart to help us as Christian mothers, daughters, sisters, and friends to come together in his name to better equip each other on our journeys in fulfilling our God-given purpose on this earth. The Bible speaks about "guarding your heart above all else, for it determines the course of your life" (Proverbs 4:23). This is only the beginning, and my prayer is that many will be equipped, healed, set free, and restored as you read and learn about yourself, life, love, and how to properly date while waiting on your godly mate. The Holy Spirit is encouraging you through this message.

Let's pray together as you begin:

> Dear Heavenly Father, in the name of Jesus, I ask that you search my heart and any questions that were left unanswered, please reveal them to me through your Word as I read this book. I ask that you expose any hidden areas of my heart that have hindered me from knowing you and serving you more effectively. I welcome any conviction of your Holy Spirit and ask for your grace to carry out what you desire of me. Father, help me keep it holy and learn how to keep it holy while I date and wait on the man who you have divinely favored me to marry and live out my life through you. Amen!

"CHANGE YOUR THOUGHTS AND YOU CHANGE YOUR WORLD."
—Norman Vincent Peale

One

What Is Dating and What It's Not?

What is dating to you? The word *dating* means different things to different people. In today's generation, it has changed from when our parents and grandparents were brought up. A dating relationship in today's time can be assumed as monogamous or open, short-term or long-term, serious or casual. While the term has several meanings, it usually refers to the act of meeting and engaging in some mutually agreed-upon social activity in public, together, as a couple.

I want you to sit back and think about how you define dating. If you can establish what dating is as a daughter of Christ, you will be able to ask the right questions about what dating is to whomever you are dating and establish a foundation that is pleasing to God.

Exercise 1
The Right Word

As a woman of integrity, which words would best describe your dating relationship? Below are some of the most commonly used words to describe dating:

- going out
- together
- talking
- being with someone
- seeing each other
- hubby-wifey status
- just friends
- friends with benefits
- getting to know one another
- courting
- hooking up

Which of these words stand out to you as unpleasing to God? Which of these words stand out to you as someone who is not honoring you and keeping it holy? Offhand, you should have crossed out "hubby-wifey status," "friends with benefits," and "hooking up." These three terms are not appropriate and are demeaning to you and your worth as a daughter of Christ.

As daughters of Christ, we must pay attention to the labels people use. You and your mate should both accept the same definition for your relationship. In this day and age, we are so used to the word *dating* that we might not be able to imagine any other approach to the relationship when, in fact, there are several. *Dating* was originally the motivation behind why a man or woman would invest time with a person: to see if he or she was a potential marriage partner. The word *dating* is used too freely with so many different meanings that we fail to ask the right questions to ensure that we are on the same page with our male mates.

I can speak firsthand about how I have gotten myself into some situations that I later regretted because I was too scared of running the boy off. I didn't want to ask him too many questions. As I have grown older and wiser, I have learned that my questions are not for them or about them. Asking questions is for you. If he doesn't like you asking questions, that is your answer. It is best to move on. I want you to know and understand that no amount of questions is too many.

Now that you have defined what dating is to you, ask yourself about the purpose of dating? Dating ought to have an honorable purpose. Its purpose was originally designed to help you—as a daughter of Christ—determine with a son of Christ whether or not you want to marry one another. When it comes to dating, Christians have to be careful not to blur the lines with secular dating. The purpose for dating is to step into a serious process of finding a spouse. I know you are way too young to be thinking about marriage now, but I don't want you to fall into the trap like I did of dating because my friends were dating, because it's fun, or because I "just wanted a boyfriend." In the secular world, people view dating as a way to get to know many people, and marriage may not play a part in the mind-set of some people. Not every person you meet will have the same intentions as you. Be sure to ask questions to ensure that you are both on the same page.

Exercise 2
Purpose or Passion: Why Do You Want to Date?

Dating is for the mature in mind. You can't have a great relationship if one or both of you are not in a mature mind-set to date. We often get so caught up in the desperation of being in love, wanting love, and seeing what we think is love that we become vulnerable. We get caught up in what we see on television, in the movies, and on the Internet. I want you to think about *your* purpose for dating. This is not about what your friends or your families think—it is about you!

I want to date because

_____

_____

_____

_____

_____

_____

_____

_____

_____

_____

_____

_____

_____

_____

_____

_____

_____

_____

> "I DON'T LIVE BY OTHER PEOPLE'S TIME
> TABLES; I LIVE BY GOD'S.
> —*Shannon L. Alder*

Two

What Time Is the Right Time?

When I was thirteen years old, I was not ready to date. I had recently accepted God as my Lord and Savior and was trying to learn God's ways. I wanted to be a good girl, and I was trying to make sure I did the right things to obey my parents. However, on the flipside, I wanted to stay cool and make sure I was still fitting in with the in crowd. I wanted to have a boyfriend because everyone else had one.

If I don't have a boyfriend, what will my peers think about me? I questioned myself all the time, wondering if I was weird or if something was wrong with me. I would constantly battle with myself and think that I would be an outcast if I didn't date. It was hard for me to navigate my emotions and feelings.

When I first entered middle school, everyone I knew was dating. I would look up to my older cousin and her friends and see how they had boyfriends. I was amazed by how their boyfriends would walk them to class and how they would hold hands. I would see them dressing like each other, getting flowers on Valentine's Day, and walking around middle school with fifteen or twenty balloons that their boyfriends got them for their birthdays. I thought, *I want that.*

The truth of the matter was that I didn't know what *that* was. I would see my cousin and her friends and think, *That is what middle school is all about.* I had no clue.

With dating, timing is everything. Ask yourself some questions: Am I old enough to date? What age is appropriate for me to start dating? Ask your parents the same questions. Your answers probably will not match up. It is appropriate to have this conversation with your parents to establish what they deem appropriate in their household. The worst thing you can do is sneak behind your parents' backs and get caught dating when the discussion determined that it was not the right time.

You may want to enjoy your youth and wisely put off dating until you feel that you are old enough to know yourself better. It's okay to admit that you're not ready or don't trust yourself to make such a big decision. It is okay to say, "When I feel that my personality has been stable for a couple of years, then I will start thinking about dating." When you are ready, you are ready. Don't rush the process. This book is about helping you make better choices and finding positive influences to help you along the way.

Don't be like me and get caught up with the hoopla and the hype of dating and having a boyfriend, especially because everyone else has one. Everyone else may not be saved. Everyone else may not have a relationship with God. Not everyone is a princess of the Heavenly Father. Ask God to reveal to you the appropriate time to start dating. Let us pray:

> God, thank you for this season of understanding. Thank you for opening my eyes to see that I can't do anything without you. With that understanding, I know that I have to seek your council with all matters in my life. As I am learning and growing,

I understand that your ways are not of this world. I am asking you if it's okay for me to date. Am I ready? Allow me to see why I want to date and to make sure that I am not doing it to please others. I want to follow your ways—and I solely want to please you. Amen!

Three

It's All About You

In my preteen stage, I remember being teased by my cousins all the time about being, "Ms. Goody Two-Shoes," the suck-up, the outcast, and the one who didn't like to get in trouble. I never fit in with what they were doing, especially if I knew I was going to get in trouble for it. I preferred spending time with my grandma and hanging with her all day or going to church.

Oftentimes because I dare to be different, I didn't fit in. I considered myself the watcher, the one who liked to learn from other people's mistakes, the smart one (even though my cousins would say I was the dumb one), and the one who wasn't going to get in trouble on account of someone else.

When I turned thirteen, I began to change. When it came to liking a boy, I would find myself altering who I was just to get the boy I had a crush on to notice me. If he liked football, I would say that I liked football. If he liked the Miami Dolphins, I would say that I liked the Miami Dolphins. The sad thing is that I don't watch football now and couldn't care less about who or what is playing because the only reason I watched football back then was because the guy I was interested in was watching football. I felt like he wouldn't like me if I didn't watch football—and he would want to date the girl who watched football instead of me.

Through my studies and learning, I have learned who I am in Christ.

> For you did form my inward parts; you did knit me together in my mother's womb. I will confess and praise you for you are fearful and wonderful and for the awful wonder of my birth! Wonderful are your works, and that my inner self knows right well. My frame was not hidden from You when I was being formed in secret [and] intricately and curiously wrought [as if embroidered with various colors] in the depths of the earth [a region of darkness and mystery]. Your eyes saw my unformed substance, and in your book all the days [of my life] were written before ever they took shape, when as yet there was none of them. (Psalms 139:13–16, AMP)

He's telling us that he knew us before we were formed in our mother's wombs and that he made us fearful and wonderful. I have learned to seek him first so that he can give me insight into who I am through him and what I will I be through him. I am supposed to love me first. I am supposed to honor me first. I am not supposed to cheat on myself and push what is important to me away just to get some boy to like me.

God knows what we need before we even open our mouths to ask him for it. By trying to change what he made fearful and wonderful (ourselves), we are not giving him praise and glory for the wonder of our births. We are blessed to be here.

Knowing you is liking you. You must learn and get to know yourself before finding the ideal partner. That takes time. If you can't master the process of dating yourself and getting to know your likes and dislikes, how can you expect someone else to get to know you? What do you know about yourself? What do you like about yourself? What are some things that God is working with you on? What is he helping you change about yourself? Spending time with yourself will allow you to get to know your likes, dislikes, deal breakers, and what God has in store for your life. Marriage is one of them, but I am sure God has a bigger picture for your life besides that.

The saddest thing you can do to yourself is start off your dating journey with a long-term relationship and you're lost in your boyfriend. You know his favorite color, favorite food, favorite film, favorite everything, but when you break up, you realize that you know very little about yourself.

I have seen many girls spending most of their time and energy finding out about their boyfriends' likes and dislikes, molding themselves into what suited them. Later, they snap out of that dream of love and being in love and wake up to realize that they forgot about themselves.

I encourage you to learn about yourself. Close your eyes, dig deep into yourself and your feelings, and find out what makes you who you are.

> In whom also we have obtained an inheritance, being predestinated according to the purpose of him who worketh all things after the counsel of his own will. (Ephesians 1:11)

God chose us in advance—how awesome is that? Wouldn't you want to learn about yourself just as God knows and created you?

Exercise 3
Getting to Know Me: Who Am I?

1. What is love to me?

    o   spiritual
    o   emotional
    o   physical
    o   mental
    o   a misconception

2. What type of music do I like?

    _____

3. My best friends:

    _____

4. My favorite movie:

    _____

5. My favorite book:

    _____

6. My favorite food:

    _____

7. My favorite television show:

    _____

8. Things that drive me crazy:

    _____

    _____

    _____

9. What makes me laugh the most?

    _____

    _____

    _____

10. What makes me really angry?

_____

_____

_____

11. What makes me cry?

_____

_____

_____

12. My favorite flower:

_____

13. Things that make me smile:

_____

_____

_____

14. Things that make me sad:

_____

_____

_____

15. My favorite actor:

_____

16. My favorite actress:

_____

17. My favorite music group:

_____

18. My favorite color:

_____

19. My favorite family member:

_____

20. Three things about me that I am proudest of:

  o _____
  o _____
  o _____

21. Three things I hate to admit about myself:

  o _____
  o _____
  o _____

22. How I feel about surprises:

  _____
  _____
  _____

23. One thing I would change about the world:

  _____

24. My favorite superhero and why?

  _____
  _____
  _____

25. My biggest fear:

  _____
  _____
  _____

26. The coolest thing on my smartphone or tablet:

  _____

27. The most extraordinary thing about me that I would scream out to the world about myself:

  _____
  _____
  _____

Now that you have examined yourself and answered some solid questions about yourself, hold fast to what is true to you. Don't change yourself to get a boy you like. Learning, growing, and getting to know yourself are fine. You are becoming an individual—and that's part of learning who you are. It's all about you. Embrace this time with yourself.

What do I value?

_____

_____

_____

_____

What's best about me?

_____

_____

_____

_____

What's something about me that I need to work on to be an even better me?

_____

_____

_____

_____

By doing these exercises, you have learned about who you are as young woman. You are becoming more aware of what makes you unique. You are learning to value yourself based on what you like—not based on what someone else likes or what you think someone else likes about you. The biggest area to focus on and spend time with is you!

As you get older, you will discover that your twenty-seven questions and answers will change and improve. Pay attention to yourself. You are super-important to any healthy relationship—whether it is with a young man, your parents, your friends, or your siblings.

Although you may have grown up on Cinderella, Sleeping Beauty, and Snow White, real life is not a fairy tale. You must prepare yourself for any situation. In order to do that, you must learn about yourself.

Four

Learning What Pleases God

We often find ourselves trying to please so many people, including parents, sisters, brothers, cousins, teachers, friends, and boyfriends. The list goes on and on. When I got older, I understood that the only things I needed to focus on were learning how to please God and learning what pleases him. By focusing on pleasing God, everything—and everyone else—will fall into place. Learning about yourself and the many things you like is one thing; learning what pleases God is another.

Prior to leaving for college, Bishop Williams prayed over me and said, "Seek ye first the kingdom of God, and his righteousness; and all things would be added unto you" (Matthew 6:33).

Okay. Cool. I'll just keep on praying and reading my Bible. I've got that. I am good.

I had to learn that my actions would play into me seeking God too. Since then, I have carried this scripture with me and have tried my hardest to apply it daily with my walk in Christ.

I have had to learn that pleasing God is about putting all of my trust in him—not just bits and pieces. From the time I wake up to the time I go to sleep, my life is in his hands. I am okay with that. I had to learn that my actions involve putting all my trust in God and constantly reminding myself that God doesn't need my help. He's got this—and he's got me. Have total trust in God.

> But without faith it is impossible to please God, for he who comes to God must believe that He is, and that He is a rewarder of those who diligently seek Him. (Hebrews 11:6)

Let's start with the word *faith*. In Hebrews 11:1, God says, "Now faith is the substance of things hoped for, the evidence of things not seen." God is telling us that it's impossible to please him without having faith in him.

Imagine how you would feel if your mother, father, or someone else close to you didn't have faith in you. What if your parents didn't believe you could get an A+ in math by working hard because you came home with a D the semester before? How would you feel? Imagine how God feels about everything he has done for you—and is doing for you—if you don't have faith that he can help with getting that A+.

God loves you so much that he gave his only son to save you and me. You have to learn to seek his ways— and nothing more. That's what pleases him. By letting go of your fleshly desires and making declarations out loud, you are showing God that you totally trust him to direct you and your path. You are saying, "Lord, I totally trust you," which is pleasing in his sight.

If you are reading this book with a study group, take some time to do the *trust lean* with a friend. Have your friend stand behind you, close your eyes, fall back, and yell, "Lord, I totally trust you." If you are sitting on your bed, get up, fall back on your bed, and say, "Lord,

I totally trust you." Did you feel the heaviness come off of you? If so, that's good. You have given all of you to God. Your walk, your talk, your mind, and your life are all in his hands. Now, it's up to you not to take it away from him.

Let us pray:

Lord, thank you for this time of learning what pleases you. I ask you for your forgiveness for anything I have said or done that has hurt you. Lord, forgive me. Lord, I trust you. You have been so good to me. Every day I wake up, I know that I am not doing it alone. If it wasn't for you, I know that I would not be here. Forgive me for taking you for granted—and forgive me for my selfish ways of not waiting on you and trying to do things on my own. Lord, create in me the "who do I think I am?" attitude. I cannot live without you, Lord, and I am declaring today that I don't want to live without you, Lord. As I learn and grow, help me to continuously seek your counsel—in school, at work, with family and friends, and with anyone I date until you reveal to the man you have divinely favored to find me and I am to marry. Every life decision that I have, I pray that I seek you first. I am open to receiving your guidance. Make me consciously aware of the people you place in my life—who were sent to guide me into making the right decisions in my dating life and life in general. Steer me away from the people who are not of you. I love you, Lord. Amen!

"BEING CHALLENGED IN LIFE IS INEVITABLE,
BEING DEFEATED IS OPTIONAL."
—*Roger Crawford*

Five

Deal or No Deal

Have you ever liked someone without really knowing who he was? Boom! You started dating him, but everything inside you was telling you that he was not the one. Everything was telling you to run. Maybe you started questioning yourself about why you liked him in the first place. Once you were in that situation, your emotions and feelings got the best of you—but you decided to stick around in hopes that you could change him.

That happened to me because I didn't do my homework. I looked at bits and pieces of the picture, and I did not take my time to actually study the picture. I became anxious. I got hurt because he wasn't who I thought he was—and I couldn't change him.

As you begin to date, if you see signs that are not godly in the person you are dating, then it isn't of God. Run! You cannot change anyone—let alone a young man. Remember my words: change begins with oneself. So, if a young man doesn't see a reason to change, there's no need to try to convince him to change. You will end up hurting yourself even more in the long run. I had to learn the hard way, but through God's grace and his mercy, you can pay attention to the Holy Spirit. He will lead and guide you.

It is important to discover the characteristics of the person you are interested in dating before making a commitment to him. What are your deal breakers? Ask the guy who is interested in you a few questions: "Do you know Jesus? Is he your friend? Do you have a personal relationship with him?" Watch!

As you begin to get to know him, ask him about his faith. Focus on his relationship with God—not his religion. God will definitely show you some things. Trust me. There are plenty of young men out there who believe in God, but there are definitely fewer young men who have a relationship with him. Those who have a relationship with God will treat you differently because of their convictions.

One of the ministers in my church asked, "How do you know who or what is from God? Anything or anyone that pushes you closer to God is of God, and anything or anyone who draws you away is not. Does your appetite for God grow? Do you want to love God more—or is your walk getting stale?"

I wished I had his counsel when I first was saved at thirteen and started dating. Maybe I wouldn't have made some of the mistakes I made by dating the wrong guy. Although you are young, it's okay to seek wise and godly counsel from your pastoral team as you work to keep your purity vow as you begin to date. From that conversation, I learned about other deal breakers that I wouldn't have thought of on my own. God sent Minister Norm to ask those questions, and he showed me that I need to pay attention to what direction a person or thing is trying to move me. If they are not pushing me towards God, then they are not right for me.

Find out if the young man has been born again in the Spirit of Christ and if he shares your desire for a Christlike walk. Remember that your ultimate goal as a young lady in Christ is to date or court with the goal of finding a life partner. In 2 Corinthians 6:14–18, the

Bible speaks about not partnering up with those who are unbelievers. "How can righteousness be a partner with wickedness? How can light live with darkness?" When we partner with unbelievers, it weakens our relationship with God and compromises our morals and standards.

Let's uncover your deal breakers. A deal breaker is a factor or factors that—if unresolved—would cause you or your partner to withdraw from a deal (your relationship). Please note if the following are deal breakers for you by circling "Yes" to indicate that he may not be a good fit for you.

Exercise 4
Deal Breakers: Acceptable versus Unacceptable

♥ The way he dresses
Yes ♡ No ♡

♥ Intelligence
Yes ♡ No ♡

♥ His sense of humor
Yes ♡ No ♡

♥ His musical taste
Yes ♡ No ♡

♥ He has a criminal record
Yes ♡ No ♡

♥ The way he treats his mother
Yes ♡ No ♡

♥ He disappears without telling you where he's going
Yes ♡ No ♡

♥ He neglects you publicly
Yes ♡ No ♡

♥ He believes in sex before marriage
Yes ♡ No ♡

♥ He yells at you publicly/privately
Yes ♡ No ♡

♥ Personal hygiene
Yes ♡ No ♡

♥ He doesn't support you
Yes ♡ No ♡

♥ He doesn't respect you
Yes ♡ No ♡

♥ He flirts with other girls
Yes ♡ No ♡

♥ He lies
Yes ♡ No ♡

♥ He cheats
Yes ♡ No ♡

♥ He has substance abuse problem
Yes ♡ No ♡

♥ He abuses you
Yes ♡ No ♡

♥ He criticizes you
Yes ♡ No ♡

♥ He says grace before meals
Yes ♡ No ♡

♥ He says his prayers before he goes to bed
Yes ♡ No ♡

♥ He stays up to date with current events
Yes ♡ No ♡

♥ I would get jealous if he:

_____

_____

_____

_____

_____

_____

_____

♥ What are some other deal breakers?

o _____

o _____

o _____

o _____

o _____

Six

Free to Choose

Part of being pure is choosing to be pure. This is a choice that you have to decide on your own, and it has to be a choice that comes from you alone. Your mother, father, sister, brother, relatives, and friends can't choose for you to be pure. You are free to choose, and this journey is a journey of boldness and the courage to not compromise. You set your physical and emotional limitations and stick to them.

As Christians, we believe in abstaining before marriage. I understand that it is definitely hard to walk our purity journey in a world of impurity. We have to choose how we interact with boys. We also have to be mindful of our emotions because the emotional connection is extremely important for us.

There are many ways to walk the purity journey together. For example, some of us have even vowed to take this walk a step further and have chosen to practice "no-touch love," which is a way for us to dodge getting involved in the influential passions of being with someone, which may cause us to compromise our beliefs. This means that those who practice no-touch love are not hugging, holding hands, or kissing. This is a time to simply get to know a person and spending time with him.

I am not saying no-touch love is the right thing for you. However, you have to choose to know and set your limits. As Christians, we have to look at dating as a thoughtful process that allows us to slowly get to know a person. As young girls, you must understand that you have all your life to date. However, you only have one time to lose your virginity. Choose to keep it dear. One of the worst feelings is not to have chosen at all.

You get to choose! You choose if and when you want to hold hands. You choose when you want to hug the boy you are dating. Discuss with him if and when you would like to kiss, but keep in mind your limitations and discuss them openly and honestly with him. You have to decide together to put Christ into your relationship. That starts at the beginning. You have to choose together to set limitations on psychical touching. You have to hold each other accountable.

Let's take a dive into what the Bible says about the choices we should make. If you search throughout your Bible, you will not find one single verse or reference to dating. It's not mentioned; however, it speaks very boldly and clearly on fornication, fornicating, and fornicators. Fornication by definition is when two people who are not married to each other consensually agree to have sexual intercourse with each other. In the Old Testament, Paul spoke about fornication and how it is displeasing to God:

> Finally, dear brothers and sisters, we urge you in the name of the Lord Jesus to live in a way that pleases God, as we have taught you. You live this way already, and we encourage you to do so even more. For you remember what we taught you by the authority of the Lord Jesus. God's will is for you to be holy, so stay away from all sexual sin. Then each of you will control his own body and live in holiness and honor—not in lustful passion

like the pagans who do not know God and his ways. (1 Thessalonians 4:1–5, NLT)

As a daughter of Christ, you must learn to make your boundaries clear and known, while ensuring that you are sticking to what you believe in. You have the right to choose and not compromise. Oftentimes, as you continue to learn and grow, you will discover that your emotions may get the best of you. Dating may bring a flood of emotions that can be good or bad. The most important thing to keep is your vow. Never let anyone talk you out of keeping your vow or putting you in environments that can bring about peer pressure, causing you to break your vow. You get to choose! Being in a relationship brings about changes. You are learning and growing. Luckily, you have this book to help bring up topics and questions you normally wouldn't know how to discuss with your parents, teachers, and counselors.

I longed for an avenue that I could take to gain knowledge before venturing out and trying to figure out dating on my own. It can be hard to talk to parents about this stuff. I have a great relationship with my mom. I talk to her daily, but when I was a teenager it was hard to talk to my mom or dad about dating, kissing a boy, or even holding hands with him. My dad hated that I was starting to date in high school, which wasn't bad since most of my peers were already dating in middle school. The choices I made during that time weren't the best because I was choosing to do what my peers were doing. I was choosing to base my relationship on things that were superficial. That's why choosing the right environments are important. Being in the wrong place at the wrong time can make it difficult to stick to your beliefs and your vow.

The enemy is waiting for us to fall into temptations.

However, if you understand how to prevent temptation from getting the best of you, you will continue to hold true to the vow you made to God and keep yourself pure. Do not put yourself in situations where you could fall into temptations. You get to choose!

Seven

Resisting Temptation

Temptation represents the strong urge or desire to have or do something unwise or wrong. That's why you must have a plan in place to ensure that you don't fall into temptation and learn to find ways to resist it. Temptation comes from many avenues in life. It comes from the images that enter our eyes through movies and television shows. It comes from the music we listen to. It comes from how we dress, where we go on dates, and even our desires. Temptations are all around us.

As Christians, God has given us the power to resist. For example, if you find that being alone with a young man is a temptation problem, you need to learn how to come up with ways to not end up alone with him. You could go on group dates or activities with your friends or go out during the day in public places.

In Matthew 26:41 the Bible says, "Keep watching and praying that you may not enter into temptation; the spirit is willing, but the flesh is weak." As a Christian young woman, you have to be smarter and a lot more careful if you are maintaining your purity and saving yourself for marriage. You have to be careful about what you allow to enter your eyes and ears. You have to pay attention to your motives and the reasons behind your actions. Above all, you need to pray continuously.

During my journey, temptation fell on me because my desires with dating were wrong. My thoughts, influences, and mind-set were wrong. I wanted to date because I saw everyone else dating. I was following what they were doing instead of following God. Since I did not put on the full armor of God, I fell into temptation. My desires were not of God because I was trying to fit in.

As you are beginning your dating journey, make sure that you protect your mind and thoughts with (images of) things of God—not of the world or lustful desires. If your desires are not godly, maybe you should hold off on dating until you fully examine why you want to date and whether you are ready to date. You may want to pray and ask God to help with rechanneling your desires. "You do not belong to yourself, for God bought you with a high price. So you must honor God with your body" (1 Corinthians 6:20).

I want you to come up with some non-tempting dating ideas and environments that you can participate in and not be tempted. By writing them down, you are strategizing a plan so that you won't fall into temptation when you are out on a date.

Exercise 5
Non-Tempting Dating Ideas and Environments

♥ Date 1: Where would you go and what would you do?

_____
_____
_____

♥ Date 2: Where would you go and what would you do?

_____
_____
_____

♥ Date 3: Where would you go and what would you do?

_____
_____
_____

♥ Date 4: Where would you go and what would you do?

_____
_____
_____

♥ Date 5: Where would you go and what would you do?

_____
_____
_____

♥ How was your first date?

_____
_____
_____

♥ Who did you go out with? _____

♥ Did any of your deal breakers come up?

_____

_____

_____

♥ If yes, how do you feel?

_____

_____

_____

♥ How many dates have you been on so far?

_____

♥ What did you learn about yourself and about dating from your first three dates?

_____

_____

_____

_____

_____

♥ Did you make it to dates 4 and 5? If so, how are you feeling about the relationship you are developing?

_____

_____

_____

♥ If not, what happened? What are some things you need to look out for next time?

_____

_____

_____

♥ Now that you've been on five dates, which one was your best date?

_____

_____

_____

♥ Why was it your best date?

_____

_____

_____

♥ What are the top three dating spots you are most comfortable going to that haven't been tempting?

_____

_____

_____

Now that you have established dating spots that work best for you and your male friend, here are some suggestions: group dates at the movie theater, bowling, skating, miniature golfing, lunch with friends and family, dinner with friends and family, amusement parks, water parks, concerts, getting ice cream together, the zoo, or the park. Just remember public—and not private—is the way to go.

Temptation is real. Don't think for one second that the devil won't try to tempt you. If he tried to tempt Jesus, what makes you think that he won't try to tempt you?

> Finally, brethren, whatever things are true, whatever things are noble, whatever things are just, whatever things are pure, whatever things are lovely, whatever things are of good report, if there is any virtue and if there is anything praiseworthy—meditate on these things." (Philippians 4:8, NKJV)

Let us pray:

Lord, I am coming to you in prayer with humility by submitting myself to you. You told us in James 4:7

(NKJV), "Therefore submit to God. Resist the devil and he will flee from you." By submitting to you, I know that I can't do anything without you. I am asking for your help to resist the devil and all things that he will try to use to get me to fall into temptations as I begin my dating journey. Lord, you told me that by submitting to you and resisting the devil and his temptation, he will flee from me. I rebuke the spirit of temptation over me and my life. Help me to be watchful of the things I watch on TV or at the movies. Help me block out things that would cause me to fall into temptation—knowingly or unknowingly— whether I am seeing it, listening to it or just passing time. Lord, I am making a vow to sustain my purity until I get married. I am asking for your protection, wisdom, and grace to help me keep my vow. I pray that you remove anything that is not of you or that tries to take me off course. In your holy name, I pray. Amen!

> "WHEN WE PUT GOD FIRST, ALL OTHER THINGS
> FALL INTO THEIR PROPER PLACE OR
> DROP OUT OF OUR LIVES."
> —*Ezra Taft Benson*

Eight

And In That Order

When I was growing up, people said, "The man is the head, and the woman is the tail." In *My Big Fat Greek Wedding,* the mother said, "The man is the head, but the woman is the neck—and she can turn the head any way she wants."

As for man and woman—husband and wife—we are one. There is an order we are to follow as daughters in Christ to ensure that we are living our lives the way God intended us to live.

God, family, and then everything else is the order we should follow. You must learn the order in which you were created to be able to understand the significance of why you were created and made for this earth as a woman.

> So the Lord God caused the man to fall into a deep sleep; and while he was sleeping, he took one of the man's ribs and then closed up the place with flesh. Then the Lord God made a woman from the rib he had taken out of the man and he brought her to the man. The man said, "This is now bone of my bones and flesh of my flesh; she shall be called 'woman,' for she was taken out of man." That is why a man leaves his father and

> mother and is united to his wife, and they become
> one flesh. (Genesis 2:21–24, NIV)

In order to know who you are and where you're going, you must first learn where you come from, from whom you have come from, and why it happened that way. Genesis 2:21–24 (NIV) makes it clear that you came from God. He saw that Adam needed companionship, a partner, a friend, and a relationship.

Do you know why God chose a rib to form Eve? Do you know the purpose the ribs serve in your body? Your ribs serve as protection and support to your respiratory system, as well as other vital organs in your body. God created man to protect the woman, but as women, we are also to protect our men. If you came from the same body, you shouldn't demean, hurt, dishonor, abuse, or reject the very thing that is a part of who you are.

Men and women are to serve one another as companions as we live out our days on earth. God created Eve with the rib of Adam to signify the support they should be getting from one another as they serve one another as the vital organ of keeping the family together through God. God created Eve from the rib of Adam to show that, as a husband and a wife, we are to serve as ventilators to each other. In other words, we are to breathe on one another just as God breathes into us.

I missed this lesson and failed because I never took the time to look at the order. I never took the time to study the Bible to see my significance as God's daughter and the importance of putting God first. I wanted to know the feeling of having someone who would like me, but I never stopped to think about who I was to Christ or what I was to God. I never looked at how much I meant to him or what he wanted from me at that time in my life. I didn't consider whether he felt it was time for me to have a boyfriend.

I had to learn the hard way that the Father knows best. God knows what makes you happy. He knows what makes you sad. He knows you, and he knows that timing is everything. He told us that he created us in his own image. He told us that even the hairs on our heads are all numbered.

> Oh yes, you shaped me first inside, then out; you formed me in my mother's womb. I thank you, High God—you're breathtaking!! Body and soul, I am marvelously made! I worship in adorations— what a creation! You know my inside and out, you know every bone in my body; you know exactly how I was made, bit by bit, how I was sculpted from nothing to something. Like an open book, you watched me grow from conception to birth; all the stages of my life were spread out before you, the days of my life all prepared before I'd even lived one day. (Psalm 139:13–16, MSG)

Why wouldn't you want to seek him and his kingdom first? He sees things that you don't see, and he knows things that you don't know. Do you know that he wants the best for you? I had to learn not to lean on what I saw or what I knew. I needed to put all of my trust in him. God comes first. In your youth, you have the opportunity to gain this knowledge so that you don't put yourself in situations that you will regret later in life.

After experiencing another breakup, I worshiped, prayed, broke down, and surrendered to God. I asked him to take this cup from me. I remember telling God that he created men, he knows their intentions (good or bad). He knows what's going to work and what's not going to work within a dating relationship with me and a man. He knows who he has set to be my husband and who I am divinely meant to be partnered with. He knows how it will happen and when it will take place.

I asked why on earth I wasn't inviting God in? I asked him to teach me how to date. I asked him to teach me about me first. I asked him to show me how to keep him first and to show me when it's time for my family to be born. The order is that God is at the forefront.

"THE BEAUTY OF A WOMAN MUST BE SEEN FROM
IN HER EYES, BECAUSE THAT IS
THE DOORWAY TO HER HEART, THE PLACE
WHERE LOVE RESIDES."
—*Audrey Hepburn*

Nine

What Do I Have to Give?

I want a husband who is tall, dark, and handsome. He must be at least six feet tall, have blue or brown eyes and well-maintained hair, and smell good. He must be a lawyer, doctor, football player, or basketball player. He must make a lot of money and be like Prince Charming. Is your list similar? My favorite movie while growing up was *Ever After: A Cinderella Story* with Drew Barrymore. She spoke her mind, and the prince embraced her confidence. I wanted my love story to be just like that. However, the difference was that she knew who she was—and I had no clue.

When I started to put my trust in God—and I started to totally trust Him to guide me—he revealed to me through his word what a man of God is to look for in a woman. I understood that it's not all about what I am looking for. It's about me becoming a good thing. "Whoso findeth a wife findeth a good thing, and obtaineth favour of the Lord" (Proverbs 18:22). God is clearly telling young women of God that we are good things. I am a good thing, you are a good thing, and we all have to learn what we have to give.

You may be wondering what you bring to the table as you begin the process of transitioning into the dating world. It's not about your looks because looks fade. It's not your occupation because there are a lot of successful single women who are lawyers, doctors, sales managers, actresses, engineers, and business owners. Many of them struggle with dating and figuring out how to date with God leading them. What are you carrying inside of you? How would you describe your personality? What qualities do you carry? While you are thinking of the answers to these questions, let me define the word *good*. "Good is morally excellent; virtuous; righteous; satisfactory in quality, quantity, or degree; of high quality; excellent; right; proper; fit: well-behaved: kind, beneficent, or friendly: honorable or worthy; in good standing."

God is plainly telling us what it takes to be a wife, which is something all women of God aspire to be one day. Why are we getting caught up in what the world says a man should be and have when God clearly tells us that we are the good things? If a man finds a good thing (his wife), then he will obtain favor with God. If a man finds his wife (a good thing), he'll gain favor by having us in his life forever. God tells him that he'll obtain favor—"the state of being approved or held in regard; preferential treatment; a gift bestowed as a token of goodwill, kind regard, and love."

They should be knocking down our doors to ensure that they are properly honoring us, protecting us, and valuing us like the good things we are. How can they do this if we don't know our value, our worth, and what we are to them?

You have to learn to stay true to who you are and what makes you happy. You have to learn to embrace you. In this world, so many opinions get tossed around as far as whether to be married, a life partner (whatever that is), engaged, or single. We are battling with what we need to be and who we need to be like. These opinions come from your friends, social media, and the world in general, but the only opinion that should matter is that of God. What works for others will not work for you. God made one Beyoncé, one Kate Middleton, one Sofia Vergara, one Ayesha Curry, and one Michelle Obama. Who are you? They discovered their purposes and became "good things" (wives)—what is yours? What are your plans for setting yourself apart from the masses? What do you have to give? Set yourself up on your God-given purpose. By embracing you, the man who God divinely favors you to have will show up and know he's found a good thing (his wife).

Exercise 6
I Am Who I Am—and That's a Good Thing

♥ What are you carrying inside of you? This question is tough to answer if you do not know who you are and if you do not know your purpose as a carrier through Christ. If that is the case, stop for a moment and pray to God to reveal this to you. Come back and fill in the blank after he shows you the answer.

_____

_____

_____

_____

♥ How would you describe your personality?

_____

_____

_____

_____

♥ What good qualities do you carry?

_____

_____

_____

_____

♥ What are some areas of opportunities you may need help with? Examine yourself, pray, and ask God to open your eyes so you can see the areas that need to change in order for you to be a good thing.

_____

_____

_____

_____

"I'M A HOPELESS ROMANTIC AND I BELIEVE THAT YOU CAN FIND LOVE IN MANY DIFFERENT PLACES AND BE VERY CONFLICTED. I'VE DISCOVERED AS I'VE GROWN UP THAT LIFE IS FAR MORE COMPLICATED THAN YOU THINK IT IS WHEN YOU'RE A KID. IT ISN'T JUST A STRAIGHTFORWARD FAIRYTALE."
—*Rachel McAdams*

Ten

Don't Get Caught Up in the Fantasy of Dating

As a young girl, I thought dating was going to be so much fun. I like going to the movies, I like going to the park, I like going skating, I love eating, and I like talking on the phone. I had it all categorized as these amazing wonderful experiences. These thoughts sound good, don't they? Little girls grow up with *The Princess and the Frog, Cinderella, The Little Mermaid, Beauty and The Beast,* and *Snow White.* Those movies programed our brains to believe a man should sweep us off our feet and go to the moon and back for us. They taught us that true love is magical and wonderful. They are so happy together, and they don't fight, get into disagreements, or have any hardships in life.

As a young girl, I thought my young adult life was going to be fun, exciting, magical, and wonderful—just like in the movies. *When I grow up, I am going to date and marry my high school sweetheart, start a family with him, and live a happily ever after.* Let's just say it didn't turn out the way I thought it would. My first boyfriend and I parted ways after our first year of dating, and I didn't have a high school sweetheart.

I didn't factor in the breakups, the dishonesty, the lies, the games, and all the other stuff that happened because I didn't include God into my plans. I was too busy trying to get to my fairy tale. I had to learn the hard way that life isn't a fairy tale, but with a life through Christ, all things are possible. There will be trials and tribulations, but I am more than a conqueror. Through God, my steps are ordered.

Some parents aren't ready for their daughters to date. It's good to talk to them and discuss when the time is right in their households. Don't sneak—it's not worth it. They might not want to think about a young man liking you, at your age. You may have already had the conversation with them, and they don't mind you dating (as long as they know him and his family). The best thing you can do is have the conversation. In the real world, parents are set in place to protect you.

As daughters of Christ, we can't see dating the way that the world sees dating. We have to read stories from the Bible that can teach us the ways to live our lives through Christ. Let's take a look at some of the love stories in the Bible:

- ♥ Adam and Eve: God saw that Adam needed a mate (just as he gave mates to the animals). For that, God told him that he would make him a helpmeet.
- ♥ Abram and Sarai (Sara): When Abram was directed by God to leave his family and go to an unknown land, Sarai followed him. She didn't ask why, who, how, what, or any of the other questions that ladies tend to ask. By being with Abram—a man fully trusting in God and his Word—she was rewarded by giving birth to Isaac.

♥ Jacob and Rachel: Jacob served fourteen years for Rachel. In the end of it all, God blessed Rachel— and she gave birth to Joseph.

♥ Boaz and Ruth: Ruth was a widow who promised to take care of her mother-in-law (Naomi), because of her loyalty she told Naomi. "Whither thou goest, I will go; and where thou lodgest, I will lodge: your people will be my people, and your God will be my God." With her loyalty to follow Naomi, Ruth returned to Bethlehem-Judah. Ruth ended up marrying Boaz. Boaz looked at Ruth favorably. He had Ruth's best interests at heart and did all he could to ensure her safety—just as she did for Naomi.

♥ The greatest love story of them all is Jesus: God gave his only Son, and Jesus died for you and me.

Relationships are important to God. As we love each other, we are showing the love of God. That's why relationships are important to him. These stories show how the learning points include God in the process. These people totally trusted him. There is giving and taking. There is pressing and shaking. There will be tears and times when you don't understand. In the end, there will be triumphs and victories because God was in the center of it all.

In my youth, I was so focused on what everyone else was doing in the world. Had I taken the time to study and learn my Bible, I would have known better than to think I could date without God being present. It's more than the birds, the bees, and all the magical things they show us in fairy tales. I wouldn't have struggled the way I did. I wouldn't have cried the tears I cried. I wouldn't have done some of the things I did that weren't pleasing to God or showing my purpose through Him.

"THE FLOWER WHICH IS SINGLE NEED NOT ENVY
THE THORNS THAT ARE NUMEROUS."
—*Rabindranath Tagore*

Eleven

Worry about Yourself

People are so funny, and I am including myself. We are always looking at what others have and comparing it to what we have. I know firsthand that comparing is not good for you or me. *Comparing* means "to estimate, measure, or note the similarity or dissimilarity between a person, place, or thing of which we are trying to compare."

We are always looking at others and trying to figure out how we measure up to what the world says we should look like, be like, think like, talk like, and walk like. In Galatians 5:25–26 (MSG), Paul tells us that this is the kind of life we have chosen. We live the life of the Holy Spirit—let us make sure that we do not just hold it as an idea in our heads or a sentiment in our hearts. We must work out its implications in every detail of our lives. We should not compare ourselves with others as if one of us was better and another was worse. We have far more interesting things to do with our lives. Each of us is an original.

As I was discovering who I was as a young woman and figuring out what I aimed to be as an adult, my dad told me that I should be like someone else. He would always tell me that I needed to be more like "that person," and I hated it. It irritated me when people would tell me I looked like someone else, talked like someone else, or acted like someone else. I battled with myself, thinking that something must be wrong with me—with the person God was cultivating me to be. I would beat myself up about how I looked and wonder why my body wasn't shaped like the other girls. I didn't know why I learned differently than the next person, what the next girl had that I didn't have, or why the boys liked her more than me. Everyone thinks that way.

We are all fearfully and wonderfully made. There is no need to be a duplicate of your mother, father, cousins, friends, the girlfriend of the boy you secretly have a crush on, or anyone else. You are who you are for a reason. That's why you are short, tall, skinny, thick, full figured, or have long hair or short hair. All of us are born with a purpose. Paul told us that we have chosen the life of the Spirit. No matter what trendy things the world gets caught up in—clothes, shoes, guys who drive fast cars, big houses, big butts, or full lips—we do not need to participate in it because we are all original.

Exercise 7
I Am Staying in My Lane—Just Drive!

♥ What are some things that set you apart from others? Why are you an original?

_____

_____

_____

_____

_____

♥ What are you passionate about?

_____

_____

_____

_____

_____

♥ When you are alone, what do you think about? What do you like to do when you're alone (sing, draw, write)?

_____

_____

_____

_____

_____

♥ When you look at yourself, what beauty do you see? List as many things as you can. Focus on what you see and not on what someone told you they see. Is it your smile, your eyes, or your hair?

_____

_____

_____

_____

_____

After you have answered these questions, don't ever let anyone tell you otherwise. Pray and ask God to open your eyes to see what he sees. He told us that we are fearfully and wonderfully made. Ask him to show you all the wonder in you. Remember that God created us in his image—and that's all that matters.

"THE BAD BOY: ALWAYS MORE FUN."

—*Ian McShane*

Twelve

Boys Will Be Boys

"Boys will be boys". You may hear this phrase when girls feel like they have to accept the bad behaviors of a boy they are in a relationship with. Bad boys are expected to be irresponsible, reckless, immature, undependable, careless, unreliable, boisterous, and whatever else the world decides a bad boy should be. The sad thing is that it is expected for you to be okay with that because that's what boys do. Let me set the record straight: that's a lie!

As girls, we see boys being confusing and complicated. From the time they are young, boys are running around, pulling our hair, and creating the He-Man Woman-Haters Club. When they grow into young men, they are running around, chasing us, and trying to figure out which one of us will be a good wife—or whatever their intentions may be. It's hard for us to relate to them and the way they think. It's hard to get them or understand why they do the things they do.

In grade school, some boys hit girls, picked on them, pulled their hair, or fought—and it's hard to understand what is wrong with him. You may mark them as stupid and mean—and you didn't want anything to do with them. Everyone else told you that it meant he liked you. As a young girl, your mind would be racing. *He's crazy— and so is everyone else who thinks he likes me. How can he like me when he tries to hurt me and is so mean to me?*

It makes no sense.

In second grade, I fought a boy after school because he pulled my hair. By the time I was in fifth grade, I was getting letters that said, "I like you—do you like me? Check yes or no." I responded no because he wasn't my type. My mother taught me that it shouldn't hurt when someone likes you. To this day, I make sure I follow her advice.

It's hard for young boys to channel their feelings. They fight with each other, pick on each other, and wrestle with each other—and they become best friends. In their minds, they treat the girls they like the same way they treat their best friends. They say, "Of course she's going to like me." They don't realize that a lot of girls mature faster and have totally different thought processes.

As boys mature and grow, they see how their fathers treat their mothers, how their grandfathers treat their grandmothers, and how their older brothers and cousins treat their girlfriends. That's what they mimic. "It worked for my dad. He got my mom, and she's okay with how he treats her." "It worked for my brother. He's got a fine girlfriend who lets him cheat on her, and she stays." They think the same strategy is going to work for them.

The world has a certain image of a bad boy. He's typically a fine, tall, muscular, cocky, arrogant, well-dressed jerk. Those are the guys who many good girls tend to fall for. I guess we like the drama that the bad boys bring into our lives because of their emotional issues. I can tell you firsthand that you don't want the drama that a bad boy brings.

I had a big crush on a bad boy. I saw how he treated other girls, but I had it in my mind that I could change him. If he saw that I was a good girl, he wouldn't want to mess with the other girls. We would flirt with each all the time, and he would walk me to my class every now and then. The flipside was that he was walking another girl to class too. He didn't care about my feelings or the other girl's feelings because, in his mind, he wasn't seriously dating either of us. It was like he was going to see who would be willing to do whatever it took to get him. I eventually gave up, but during that time, I questioned myself and my self-worth.

Pay attention to his actions toward you. Some actions may be good, and others may be bad. One day, he may tell you how beautiful you are, but the next day, he's saying the same thing to another girl. He may walk you to class one day and walk right past you without saying a word the next day. You may spend your days and nights on the phone with him—and then he disappears for three days. He stops answering your phone calls and text messages. This is a classic move of a bad boy. When you do get a hold of him, he'll act like you are the crazy one. Bad boys are calculating, and they will always put you on an emotional roller coaster.

All a bad boy needs is for you to get emotionally attached. He'll try to figure out how you are going to emotionally accept his bad behavior. He may be talking on the phone and have you thinking that you are forming a relationship—only to find out that he was also talking to the girl who lives right next door to you.

A bad boy lives for the thrill of how long he can go without getting caught. When he does get caught, he might say, "She's just a friend," "When did we become official?" or "We're not in a relationship."

The enemy wants you to think that bad boys are so much cooler than the boys with integrity. Some people say that boys with integrity are boring, but they're not. God is calling you higher than bad boys. In the long run, God is saving you from heartache and pain. In my experiences, bad boys aren't what they're cracked up to be. They are selfish, mean, and nasty, and they will not honor or protect you. I've heard the phrase, "Hurt people hurt people," and a bad boy is no exception.

I thought it was cute that he would act like a jerk at times or could be a butt because I could too. As long as his attitude wasn't directed toward me, I was good. He was not the exception to the rule. He would play games, and I would play games back. The games get old very quickly. I looked at it as a challenge that I would win because I lacked knowledge of who I was in Christ.

I was a good girl. I was a church girl. I wasn't like the rest of the girls who didn't grow up in church. I would think, *I am one of God's daughters, and he better treat me right.* Bad boys don't care about that. It's all about them. A bad boy feels like you should take it as a privilege to even be talking to him in the first place, especially if you are high on their roster and not on the sideline and waiting to get in the game.

It's not okay to settle! You should never accept a bad boy's behavior or mistreatment in any manner. That's where this world gets it wrong in the first place. The world has accepted that boys will be boys. As daughters of God, we have to take a stance. We have to say no to bad behavior. Too many girls chase after boys and accept their bad behavior.

In exercise 8, take some time to see if you are dating a bad boy—or if you are in the process of starting a relationship with one. Keep in mind that you are looking at a combination of responses. Don't stress yourself out if he does one or two of these things. You will know if these things happen a lot during your interactions.

Exercise 8
He Tried It!

Check all that you may have heard before.

♥ He tells you that he's going to call, but he doesn't call you, text you, or video chat you. If you have heard the following before, he tried it! (You may not be the only one he's talking to.)

o   I fell asleep.
o   I was tired.
o   I forget.
o   I was busy.
o   My phone died.

♥ He tells you that he doesn't like to take pictures. If you have heard the following before, he tried it! (He may not want to get caught or questioned about who you are in his life—or he may not want to be seen with you.)

o   You know I don't like to smile.
o   Why are you always taking pictures?
o   I am not a photogenic person.
o   Don't take my picture.
o   I am a private person.

♥ He tells you that he's not into social media. If you have heard the following before, he tried it! (This is because he may not want you to see who he knows, what he's doing, where he's been, or who he's been with.)

o   Facebook is nothing but drama.
o   I don't want my face on all those sites.
o   I don't want all those people in my business.

- o You don't have to let everyone know what we do.
- o As long as you know I am with you, I don't need to be on Facebook.

♥ You've never met his family or friends. If you have heard the following before, he tried it! (This is because he's hiding you and doesn't want his family and friends to know that he's with you because you are not his main girlfriend.)

- o I don't want them in our business.
- o You know it's you and me. Who cares about the other people?
- o It's all about you and me. We don't need our friends in our business.
- o You wouldn't want to meet them.
- o I don't take girls around my family like that.

♥ He says things that make you feel insecure or less than what you are. If you have heard the following before, he tried it! (This is because he has a superiority complex and feels insecure.

- o You could stand to lose some weight
- o If only you'd look like the video girls, you'd be a ten.
- o Man, you are so skinny.
- o You say some dumb stuff.
- o You talk too much.
- o Why are you dressing like that?
- o You need some meat on your bones.
- o Girls can be so dumb sometimes.

♥ You have never been on a real date with him, and he never wants to do anything outside of talking on the phone with you. If you have heard the following before, he tried it! (This is because he doesn't want to be seen with you, and he is hiding you.)

o   I have practice (football, basketball, band, baseball, etc.).
o   I don't have any money.
o   I have to work that weekend.
o   Something came up—I have to cancel.
o   I am not going to be able to make it.
o   I have a family situation that came up—that's why I had to cancel.

Assessment

How did it go? Do you see a pattern of bad behaviors? Each mark checked off indicates that there may be a problem. If you checked more than five, you seriously need to evaluate your relationship.

Mia's Story

I am going to end this chapter with Mia's story. Mia is a smart, loving, and kind girl who loves God, but she ended up falling for a bad boy. In the beginning, she didn't realize he was a bad boy because they went to the same church at one point. In the beginning, he was super-sweet and kind to her. Her parents knew his parents, and he seemed like a nice boy.

Derek was involved in the music ministry at her church, and Mia sang in the church choir. Derek played the piano, and he was very good at it. Derek was very handsome. All the girls loved Derek and envied Mia because, for years, Derek would try to talk to Mia. She didn't give him the time of the day because he was sixteen—and she was fourteen.

Mia's church decided to take a summer trip to New Orleans, and that's when she started to take a liking to Derek. He would open doors for her during the whole trip. He would give her his jacket if she was cold, and he even had flowers delivered to her hotel room. He was being so thoughtful, kind, and sweet to her. She thought that he couldn't be a bad guy. When they got back from their trip, Derek asked Mia's parents if he could take her out on a date. They agreed. They went to dinner and a movie for their first date. Derek was her first kiss.

Derek asked her to be his girlfriend at her fifteenth birthday dinner. Mia felt so special because he asked her in front of her family and friends. Mia accepted. It was an exciting time in their relationship. Derek was her very first boyfriend. In the beginning, it was everything she imagined dating to be. They would talk on the phone for hours and go to the movies together. They supported each other after school. She was a cheerleader, and he played football for her school's rival. They went to different church events together since they weren't going to the same church anymore.

One day, Mia got a call from a girl who asked how she knew Derek. Kate said they had been girlfriend and boyfriend for a year—and they were still together. Mia's heart dropped. She couldn't believe what was happening. She had been making plans for their six-month anniversary.

Derek denied being in a relationship with Kate. He told Mia that he had talked to Kate about a year ago—way before he had gotten serious about wanting to date Mia. He told Mia that Kate wasn't over him—and that she was mad because he didn't make her his girlfriend. Derek told Mia that she was being insecure and inexperienced. He told Mia that she was the only girl he was dating and that Kate was jealous of their relationship.

Mia thought, *How could he be cheating on me when we are spending so much time together?* A few months later, Derek started distancing himself from her. He stopped calling her every day. When they would talk, they would end up arguing about some girl, him not calling her back, or how he was treating her. Derek blamed all the relationship fails on Mia.

Mia's parents did not approve of Derek and the way he was acting toward Mia. They even suggested that they take a break from each other. He told her he was acting that way because she was trying to save herself for marriage and didn't want to take their relationship to the next level. Derek told her she was crazy for trying to keep her purity vow—and that no one was trying to do that. Derek admitted that he wasn't a virgin. If she continued wanting to save herself, he might leave her.

Mia was lost and confused. She started questioning herself and thought it was her fault that Derek was treating her the way he was.

One day, Derek picked her up after cheerleading practice and took her to get something to eat. He was being the Derek she knew and liked when they first started dating, but it didn't last long. As they were leaving the restaurant, Derek told her that he had to stop by his house to get his football gear. She knew that his parents weren't home. They had set a rule that they would not be alone while no one was home.

Mia convinced herself that it would be okay as long as she didn't go inside. Derek tried to get her to come inside, but Mia said no. He slammed the truck door and told Mia that he didn't know why he was wasting his time with her. He told her that there were plenty of girls who would want to date him because he was a football star, played music at church, and looked good too. Derek told her that she should be happy that he was dating her.

Mia cried during the whole ride home.

She continued to stay with Derek after that incident, a year later and their relationship only got worse. Another girl called Mia and said she was dating Derek. Her name was Nicole. Derek denied it. Mia didn't know what to do. Derek would tell her she was crazy for believing a girl before him. He had her call Nicole back, and he told the other girl to stop calling her. Mia was confused and contemplated losing her virginity to Derek to get her relationship back to the way it was in the beginning. By that time, they had been dating for year and a few months.

As a tear rolled down Mia's face, Mia recalled the day her and Derek's relationship ended. She had to battle with the closure of her relationship by herself. She developed insecurities because of the relationship and how Derek treated her. The day it ended she decided to surprise Derek after football practice. She wanted to bring him something to eat because he was usually hungry after practice. She wanted to do something nice to show him how much she cared for him. He was being so patient with her and her waiting and wanting to keep her purity vow.

She pulled up next to Derek's truck and noticed two people inside. When she got closer, she saw Derek making out with Nicole. Feeling devastated and heartbroken, Mia watched and waited until Derek saw her.

Derek shook his head with a smirk and pulled away, leaving her without a word. Derek avoided her calls. She cried and yelled on his voicemail, but Derek never responded. Mia felt hurt, hopeless, and distraught. She knew she couldn't do anything crazy because it was Derek's senior year—and she was heading into her junior year. Mia didn't want to talk to her parents because they had told her to leave him alone. She never saw or spoke to Derek again. It was like he vanished after breaking her heart.

Mia was not paying attention to the signs God was showing her during her relationship with Derek. Her friends did not approve of him, and her parents did not approve of him. She ignored everything they said was wrong about him.

You may not see it at first, but if the guy you are dating is a bad boy, he can't keep up the good guy act for long. Don't believe the hype. A bad boy is just what he is: bad. Nothing good comes from the word *bad*. What makes you think a bad boy is the exception to the rule? Bad is a poor quality—and that's not something that God would give.

"Become wise by walking with the wise; hang out with fools and watch your life fall to pieces" (Proverbs 13:20, MSG). You don't have time for that—or for him. Just say no to the bad boy.

Thirteen

What is Love?

Love is essential, critical, and indispensable. It is needed to live prosperous lives as daughters of God. Everyone needs love, and no one on earth can live without it.

> Love is patient, love is kind. It does not envy, it does not boast, it is not proud. It does not dishonor others, it is not self-seeking, it is not easily angered, and it keeps no record of wrongs. Love does not delight in evil but rejoices with the truth. It always protects, always trusts, always hopes, and always perseveres. Love never fails. But where there are prophecies, they will cease; where there are tongues, they will be stilled; where there is knowledge, it will pass away. And now these three remain: faith, hope and love. But the greatest of these is love. (1 Corinthians 13:4–8; 13, NIV)

In life, you will experience different forms of love. You will experience the love you have for God, the love you have for your father and mother, the love you have for your sister(s) and/or brother(s), the love you have for your friends and family, the love you have for yourself, and the love you have for the love of your life.

We have been taught that there's no greater love than the love of God. God loves us so much that he sent his one and only Son to die for our sins. If God sent his one and only Son to die for our sins so that we may live more abundantly, what makes you think he won't send the man he has favored you to have? You are his daughter, and the Father knows best. He will provide you with the best if you let him.

In this world, it is often taught that love should hurt. It is portrayed in movies and on television that it's okay to fight, it's okay for you to fail, it's okay not to trust, and it's okay for a man to disrespect you by cheating on you, calling you out of your name, using you, dishonoring you, not protecting you, or manipulating you.

I am here to tell you that it's not okay. The devil is a liar. Any boy you date should honor and protect you from pain, hurt, and shame. He's supposed to cover you. You shouldn't have girls coming up to you and stating that he's dating them too. You shouldn't be fighting over a boy or fighting for love and attention. You shouldn't have to worry about him mistreating you physically or mentally. You shouldn't have to dance and prance around for his attention.

I was trying to be everyone else. I was dancing and prancing around instead of being what God made me to be. I was thirteen, saved, and had no clue who I was or what my purpose was. I was trying to be a good girl and figure out what it meant to be saved. I wanted to date, go to the movies, and do what my peers were doing—but not until I learned what love was. I needed to find out who I was and what it felt like to be loved in a relationship. Did I really see, understand, and embrace 1 Corinthians 13:4–8; 13? I was too caught up with being with the in crowd. I ended up dating boys who I had no business dating in the first place. Gladly for me, I know that God is my redeemer. He's my knight in shining armor. He forgives, and he will never leave me or forsake me. That is the ultimate love.

God gave man specific instructions for how to love his wife. If you are dating a young man who is not following God's instructions, it is a cue to leave. You can't change a young man—and you can't raise him. That is his parents' job. If he can't love you or refuses to love you in the way he should, don't stay. That relationship is not of God. It's a distraction.

> Go all out in your love for your wives, exactly as Christ did for the church—a love marked by giving, not getting. Christ's love makes the church whole. His words evoke her beauty. Everything he does and says is designed to bring the best out of her, dressing her in dazzling white silk, radiant with holiness. (Ephesians 5:25–28, MSG)

That is how husbands ought to love their wives. They're really doing themselves a favor since they're already "one in marriage."

God is telling us that a husband's love should make us whole. It's not that we aren't already whole by ourselves—we are whole as a unit. Our husbands should love us so much that they're reminded of our beauty. Everything they do and say should bring out the best in us—washing dishes, holding hands, taking out the trash, or telling us how beautiful we are. We should be dancing, skipping, and hopping all over the place.

The love that God is telling us we should have, should make us sing about how good God is to allow us to have this type of human experience. A man's love for his wife should radiate with holiness. Doesn't that excite you? It should—and you should never settle for anything less.

"HOLD ON TO THE THOUGHT THAT NO EMOTION
LASTS FOREVER, NO MATTER HOW WONDERFUL
OR HOW TERRIBLE THE EMOTION MAY BE.
THE TEARS MAY LAST A LITTLE LONGER THAN
YOU WOULD LIKE, BUT IT WILL GET BETTER. I
PROMISE."
—*Osayi Osar-Emokpae, Because You Deserve Love*

Fourteen

This Is Not Going to Work

You may get a funny feeling or an inkling that
something is not going to work. In the church, we call it
a "discerning spirit." I like to stick with the Holy Spirit
leading me and guiding me when something or someone
is not sitting well in my spirit. It's like something in your
being is telling you that a person or a situation is not
going to work.

During my teenage years, I struggled with being
obedient to the Holy Spirit and doing what I wanted to do.
I just wanted to fit in. I just wanted to be like the normal
kids. I just wanted to see what dating was about like
the rest of my friends and cousins. God knew I wasn't a
normal kid—I was saved. He knew I wasn't ready. I needed
to find me and not look at life through someone else's lens.

I walked away from a relationship because I knew
it was not going to work. He was handsome, and I was
attracted to him. He was smart, but he was not the one.
As soon as I included God in my decision-making process
and actually prayed about the guy and the situation, I
realized why God was showing me red flags me and was
not allowing things to proceed.

I was stubborn. In some situations, I paid the price for doing what I wanted to do. When I included God in my situations, I dodged a lot of things that weren't good for me—or who God ordained me to be through him. God loves us. He wants us to be happy. He wants us to be prosperous. He wants us to include him in all aspects of our lives, especially our dating lives. When we don't, we get involved in things we shouldn't have been involved with in the first place.

Who do you need to cut out of your life? If you are battling within your heart and/or your spirit about whether or not it's time to throw in the towel and confess that something is not going to work, then this is the chapter for you. If you are dating someone that is not on the same godly wave (they are not rolling with God or walking on water with him), it may be time to walk away before it's too late.

Remember how 2 Corinthians 6:14–18 explained not being partnered with those who reject God? The boy who goes after your purity is rejecting God and the very bit of what God wants you to be: pure. You can't develop a partnership with a boy who is contradicting the Word of God. There's no partnership in that. That's just war. The enemy is trying his best to persuade you to give up the battle of purity and keeping your vow.

I can only guide you on things I wish someone had taken the time to explain to me. I wish someone had told me that everything was going to be okay. I wish someone had told me that I wasn't an outcast or weird because I was trying to save myself for marriage. I wish I had someone tell me that God had a plan for me and my life.

I am here to tell you that your feelings are your feelings—and yours alone. If whoever you are dating can't respect or help you honor the vow you made to God, you need to tell him to "get thee behind me, Satan"— because it is not going to work.

Exercise 9
Flag on the Play—Too Many Red Flags

Here's a list of a few red flags to consider as you are beginning to date and trying to stay true to your purity vow. Check off the ones that stand out to you—and reference back to the descriptions during your journey:

o *His core values are different than yours.* The world says opposites attract—but not with someone who is trying to detour you from your purity vow. Is he trying to pressure you from keeping your vow?

o *He doesn't seem proud of you.* If he is hesitant to introduce you to his friends or is reluctant to have any proof of you or that you are dating on his social media, this is a clear sign that he is ashamed of you. Do you feel like he is hiding you? Is he reluctant to be around you in public? Do you only go to certain events together?

o *He's not putting effort into the relationship.* You are the only one investing into the one-sided relationship. Do you feel that it's just you? Find someone who will make you a priority.

o *He lies.* If he is not honest and you are catching him in lies, it is a huge red flag. If there is no trust, there's definitely no relationship. Are you starting to see a pattern of him changing his stories?

o *He can't tell you he's sorry.* We are human and sometimes mess up. When that happens, both parties need to know that it's okay to apologize. If he is unwilling to accept responsibility for his wrongdoings, flag on the play. When he messes up, does he apologize?

o *He tries to change you.* Does he push you to grow faster than you are willing to just to benefit his own selfish gains? Is he treating you like his project? Is he comparing you to other girls? Does he give you ultimatums that you have to comply with or he'll leave you? Do you feel like he is not accepting you for who you are or where you are in your life?

o *He disrespects you.* You may have disagreements from time to time, but does he call you names or threaten you? You need to make sure you tell someone. Is he verbally or physically abusive? The first time is the last time. Once is definitely too many—flag on the play.

o *Your family and friends don't like him.* Your family and friends know you better than you think. They often see things you don't necessarily see. If no one is getting along with him—or if your parents don't like him—this is a major red flag. Does he get along with your family? If not, it may be time to go.

o *Does he get along with your friends?*

If you checked three or more red flags, it's time to move on.

Fifteen

Can I Trust You?

Trust is so important in a relationship. "Can I Trust You?" We learn to build our relationships on this one question. This is a question that God is asking you. He's asking if he can trust you to trust him. Can he trust you to let him lead you, to let him guide you, to allow him to place the right person in your life, and you not try to take control or put your trust in your heart or ordinary humans.

God posed that same question to me. Once I got it, I realized that I can't do anything without God. I cried out to him and told him to take this cup from me. I told him I couldn't do it on my own and that I totally trusted him. I realized that he knows the heart of a boy. He knows their intentions before we can even imagine what their intentions are. He knows their hearts and their thoughts. He can see them for who they are and what they are—long before our natural eyes can. Think about all the heartaches we could avoid by including God first. Trust him instead of your heart or your feelings.

> Cursed is the strong one who depends on the mere humans, who thinks he can make it on the muscle alone and sets God aside as dead weight. He's like tumbleweed on the prairie, out of touch with the good earth. He lives rootless and aimless

in a land where nothing grows. But blessed is the man who trusts me, God, the woman who sticks with God. They're like trees replanted in Eden, putting down roots near the rivers—Never a worry through the hottest of summers, never dropping a leaf, Serene and calm through droughts, bearing fresh fruit every season. The heart is hopelessly dark and deceitful, a puzzle that no one can figure out. But I, God, search the heart and examine the mind. I get to the heart of the human. I get to the root of things. I treat them as they really are, not as they pretend to be. (Jeremiah 17:5–10, MSG)

In all my relationships, I did not receive a clear view of who I needed to focus on until my late twenties. I was looking for what I liked, what my eyes found attractive, what my mind and heart were telling me I should feel like, and why I should be feeling the way I was feeling. I was selfish. I was looking at whether or not he was tall enough, athletic enough, and attractive enough, and smart enough. Could I talk to him without being bored out of my mind? Who was he hanging out with? Was he in the same crowds that I was in?

If a boy told me that he believed in God, I would get so excited. If he told me that he went to church, I would get super-excited because I thought only good boys went to church. I had no clue. I never took the time to fact-check or look at his relationship with God. I didn't talk to God about him. I was too busy talking to my friends. I was too busy thinking about our next date, how exciting it was to be dating someone, how fun it was to go on dates and get dressed up, or how good we looked together.

Boom! Let the real boy stand up—and he surely did. The same cycle repeated and left me devastated, heartbroken, and sad. I never consulted God.

> Like a cowbird that cheats by laying its eggs in another bird's nest is the person that gets rich by cheating. When the eggs hatch, the deceit is exposed. What a fool he'll look like then! (Jeremiah 17:11)

My biggest mistake was not realizing that I wasn't including God in my decision-making processes. Because of that, the relationships were destined to fail. They failed every time because I was not putting my trust in God. I paid the price for that. I ended up hurt, disappointed, and broken. I had no clue and no business with half the boys I dated. I put up a massive wall with guard dogs and barbed wire around my heart because I trusted the boys I dated instead of God.

> "NO WOMAN WANTS TO BE IN SUBMISSION TO A
> MAN WHO ISN'T IN SUBMISSION TO GOD!"
> —*T. D. Jakes*

Sixteen

The Strongest Man Wins

We all have choices, and they have causes and effects. God will drop signs along the way, but it's up to us to pick them up. I saw the signs, but I would walk right by them because I wanted to do my own thing. I felt like I was in control. If a boy wasn't fully what I wanted him to be, I thought I had the power to change him or the situation. This was the lie that I told myself and believed it was true—and I failed every time.

God is not going to force you to choose. He will be there during the selection process. If you are humble and open enough to follow him as he is directing you to the best choice for you, you will win every time. He is not going to force you to do anything that you don't want to do. Be prepared for the effects that may come along with the choices you make.

When you are choosing a boy to date, consider more than his looks. Look at his substance. You are dedicating your time to him. If he is lacking substance and submission to God, he's not winning—and he is not ready for a daughter of God. Don't settle. Substance can be defined in so many ways: being stable, dependable, and honest. Is he structured? Does he fully submit to God? Does he live his life out with God? That's more important than him being six feet tall or having a great smile with crystal-white teeth.

Looking at the fabric of a boy who is developing into a man is so important when you are choosing a boy to date. Make sure he will honor and protect you as you are beginning the dating phase of your life. The way he walks and the way he talks is a reflection of who he is and where he is in Christ. Has he sought God and asked him about you and the dating situation? Some boys are slower than others with upholding good, godly characteristics. They are also battling with right and wrong and finding out who they are. With those boys, you will have to decide whether or not they are dateable. You cannot change them—so don't waste your time trying.

A boy's fabric represents the fibers that are woven together to make the final product. These characteristics will make a godly man who is winning the battle of life and going through his processes by submitting to God. Is he trying to date you for the right reasons?

His characteristics are the fibers that make him who he is. If some of his characteristics are not appealing to you, it's okay to let him know that you are not interested. Is he honest and loyal? Is he neat, motivating, and respectful? Does he have a positive attitude? These behaviors may be near and dear to you. These are the signs to look for in a submitted young man who has a relationship with God.

Exercise 10
The Right Fabric: Character Is Key!

Do you remember when you dreamed about what your future husband would be like? Take some time to write down some of those characteristics. (List some of his features too—it's good to know what you think you might like).

♥ _____
♥ _____
♥ _____
♥ _____
♥ _____
♥ _____
♥ _____
♥ _____
♥ _____
♥ _____
♥ _____
♥ _____
♥ _____
♥ _____
♥ _____
♥ _____

The characteristics you listed are wants and desires—there's nothing wrong with that. Look at the bigger picture. I missed the bigger picture and had to go back and reexamine it.

Create a vision and make it clear. "For the vision is yet for an appointed time, but at the end it shall speak, and not lie: though it tarry, wait for it; because it will surely come, it will not tarry" (Habakkuk 2:3, KJV).

You will not get everything on your list. Right now, you probably don't know all your needs for your future husband. "But my God shall supply all your needs according to his riches in glory by Christ Jesus" (Philippians 4:19, KJV).

God told us to make every request known unto him—and that's exactly what you did. I wanted you to make your requests known. God knows what you need more than anyone else on this earth, including yourself. Sometimes those wants are the very things we don't need.

Take a look at your list. Do you see God in the midst of your wants? If so, good for you. If not, don't worry. We're going to dive into the list to make sure the husband you want to spend the rest of your life with has certain characteristics. Does he know God? Does he know the importance of submitting to God? "Do not be anxious about anything, but in every situation, by prayer and petition, with thanksgiving, present your request to God" (Philippians 4:6, NIV).

Do not be anxious about anything. I was so anxious to wait on God and see God in my dating relationships. I was so focused on my wants that I didn't stop to see or try to understand what I truly needed through God's eyes.

God guides us and shows us what the fabric of a boy of God should entail. Some of his fabric components should have strength, bravery, and courageousness. "And I sought a man among them who should build up the wall and stand in the gap before Me for [the sake of] the land, that I would not destroy it, but I found none [not even one]" (Ezekiel 22:30, AMP).

He should be filling in the gaps in life where the enemy is trying to attack you and cover you. The one who is trying to destroy your wall is not the strongest man—and he should not be winning. With the boy you are dating, you should not have the feeling of lack. You should not be lacking the support needed to be the best you that you can be in the relationship.

Let the strongest man win. Don't ever let anyone tell you that you're not good enough—or even make you feel that way. You should never feel that you are in competition with your mate because you are the prize. "Many a man proclaims his own loving-kindness and goodness, but a faithful man who can find? The righteous man walks in his integrity; blessed (happy, fortunate, and enviable) are his children after him" (Proverbs 20:6–7, AMP). Ask God to help you see the godly fabric in the spirit of the young man you are dating and show you his characteristic of submission to God.

Let us pray:

> God, thank you! Thank you for your love and kindness. You have truly showed favor on me and my life by blessing me with this guide. You taught me that I will perish with the lack of knowledge. Thank you for giving this knowledge as I continue to grow with you, in the dating phase of my life. You told me in Proverbs 19:2 (NIV), "Desire without knowledge is not good—how much more will hasty feet miss the way!" Lord, help me not to be anxious, but with my whole life seek you first. Thank you for giving me the way and showing me what the fabric of a strong boy in Christ should carry. Help me to not get distracted with the fluff, but look at his substance and the main substance is you. Amen!

> "PURITY IS THE GATEKEEPER FOR EVERYTHING
> PRECIOUS AND BLISSFUL IN GOD'S KINGDOM."
> —*Eric Ludy*

Seventeen

Blessed Are the Ones Who Keep Their Purity Vow

You are beautiful, you are precious, and you are pure. There's nothing wrong with that—or you—so don't let anyone tell you otherwise. Staying pure is everything; don't let this world trick you into thinking it's not. I know how it feels to be labeled as an outcast because all your friends are losing their virginities. The worst feeling is people looking at you as if something is wrong with you.

I know how it feels to be looked at as a "Goody Two-Shoes." I know what it's like to be teased about your belief in keeping yourself pure and wanting to please God by keeping your vow of purity. I know the feeling of disappointment of breaking the vow you made, and I can honestly say that it wasn't worth it. You don't want to waste it on a bad boy or any boy who doesn't respect your vow. At the end of the day, he will check you off his list and keep it moving, leaving you emotionally attached, hurt, and broken.

Purity is going to require you to have God's strength. Remaining pure is going to rely on you seeking God and putting him first. It involves working with God and following the Holy Spirit to lead you and guide you. Staying pure with God's strength is allowing his grace and mercy to help you wait for your God-sent prince.

God will send him to honor, respect, and protect you. You have your whole life ahead of you— enjoy it. When you are married, it will be worth the wait.

I understand what it is like to grow up in a church. The topics that the pastors are preaching may not be relatable to what's going in your young life. I understand the feeling of being misunderstood and not having someone to guide you through your emotions and feelings. I didn't have the guidance to help me channel what was going on outside the church walls when it came to dating—but now you do. I struggled to fit in and please God. The pressures of this world are so hard to manage, especially when you're in middle school, high school, or college. Trying to stay in the in crowd can be overwhelming when you are trying to do the right things.

Purity is a choice that you have to choose from your heart. With this vow, you are declaring to the world that you will remain pure until after you are married. You are making a declaration that you will live a life of abstaining from sex. You are embracing a lifestyle that will keep you pure until you are married.

Continue to fight the battle of keeping your vow and remaining pure because God knows you are amazing, strong, and courageous. That's all that matters. The Song of Solomon describes a pure woman, how wonderful she is, and as a husband how happy he was of her keeping her purity vow.

> There's no one like her on earth, never has been, never will be. She's a woman beyond compare. My dove is perfection, Pure and innocent as the day she was born, and cradled in joy by her mother. Everyone who came by to see her exclaimed and admired her—All the fathers and mothers, the

neighbors and friends, blessed and praised her.
(Song of Solomon 6:8–9, MSG)

By keeping your vow, you will be blessed and praised.
You didn't let the world trick you. If the boy you are
dating can't respect that, then he's not the one for you.
Let him go! You will be saving yourself from the hurt, the
pain, the guilt, and the shame I had because I wanted
to do it my way without including God.

Purity is not a fad. It is a daily, weekly, monthly,
yearly decision you will make until you are married. This
is moment-by-moment, second-by-second, and minute-
by-minute fight that you will consistently encounter. You
will have to rebuke yourself, the devil, your heart, and
all things that will be put in place to tempt you. That's
why God's strength and your heart's decision have to be
in order.

It's funny how God speaks to us through the Bible.
The sad thing is that we miss it because we are too
busy worrying about what's going on in the world and
our lives. When I invited God into my dating process, he
began to show me what dating would be like with him—
and how we should navigate through it with his Word.

> And that means killing off everything connected
> with that way of death: sexual promiscuity,
> impurity, lust, doing whatever you feel like
> whenever you feel like it, and grabbing whatever
> attracts your fancy. (Colossians 3:5, MSG)

Doing whatever you feel like whenever you feel like it is
going to lead you to one place: hurt. I thought I knew it
all, but I didn't. I thought I was smarter, but I wasn't. I
chose to play the game of thinking I could change the
boy instead of walking away. He may be "fine as all get

out," but if he's not walking the same godly walk or talking the same godly talk, then he wasn't sent by God. He was sent by the enemy to do damage.

In Titus 2:12 (NIV), Paul the apostle teaches us to say no to ungodliness and worldly passions, and to live self-controlled, upright, and godly lives in this present age. That is a life of purity. As a daughter of Christ, you are to push toward a life of purity—and your motives should be pure as well.

My motives were all over the place. I wanted to date because everyone else was dating. I wanted to date because my older cousins and friends were dating. I wanted to say I had a boyfriend. I didn't include God in the process. The outcome was as expected; thankfully, God is a redeemer.

Dating is more than sex. Sex is nothing when it's not with someone who values, loves, honors, protects, and respects you. That's why it's best to enjoy your youth and when that "man" finds you, when you have developed into a "woman," and when you are married, you will become one. Sex is more than the physical connection—it's a soul connection.

> There's more to sex than mere skin on skin. Sex is as much spiritual mystery as physical fact. As written in Scripture, "The two become one." Since we want to become spiritually one with the Master, we must not pursue the kind of sex that avoids commitment and intimacy, leaving us more lonely than ever—the kind of sex that can never "become one." There is a sense in which sexual sins are different from all others. In sexual sin we violate the sacredness of our own bodies, these bodies that were made for God-given and God-modeled love, for "becoming one" with another. Or

didn't you realize that your body is a sacred place, the place of the Holy Spirit? Don't you see that you can't live however you please; squandering what God paid such a high price for? The physical part of you is not some piece of property belonging to the spiritual part of you. God owns the whole works. So let people see God in and through your body. (1 Corinthians 6:16–20, MSG)

You are beautiful, you are precious, and you are pure. Own it! Know that you can still date and keep your vow. The key to your success is keeping God first and not letting anyone tell you anything different.

God gave me a vision of substance. As you begin dating, look at the substance. Do not focus so much on how you feel. Feelings fade.

As I am writing this book, I am in the process of inquiring about purchasing a home. During this journey, a question came to me in a dream: "Would you purchase your house sight unseen?"

My response was a quick and clear *No*.

God said, "Would you buy a house without receiving the deed (a deed is a legal document that is signed and delivered, especially one regarding the ownership of property or legal right)?" My response was *No*. Without the deed; I wouldn't legally own the house. Legally, I wouldn't have any right to the property."

He asked, "Then why would you give away your virtue—your purity—without being married?"

He was right. I shouldn't. Legally, I wouldn't have any rights. He can come and go as he pleases—and I would have no rights or say.

God went a little deeper and showed me a land surveyor out examining land and a home inspector thoroughly inspecting the home. Both of these jobs are extremely important to the home owner and the property owner. The land surveyor establishes boundaries to satisfy ownership and provide concrete research for legal documents. They carry out a variety of measurements dealing with the earth (ground), air, and water surfaces.

The home inspector goes through the house from the top to the bottom and looks for anything that is not right with a home and they report it. God is the inspector and the surveyor of your life and your relationships. He looks for substance. He inspects and surveys what's good or bad for you and your purpose.

God will show you signs that will tell you if you and the guy you are dating are a good fit. He will show you qualities that are not godly, and he will show you his findings through your family and friends (good or bad). He will tell you the things you want to hear and the things you don't want to hear. It's up to you to listen.

I didn't pay attention to substance. I didn't want to see that fact that my family and friends didn't like him. I didn't pay attention to God and the signs that he was showing me. I failed. I failed because I wanted to fit in. I put the pressures of fitting in before God. I failed because I was in love with the feeling of being in love and falling in love. I failed because I thought I could change him. I failed because I was looking for my happily ever after in a human instead of God.

God redeemed me and purified me again. He showed me that substance trumps looks every time. Looks will fade, but the substance will remain. The substance will sustain the relationship.

My Vow of Purity

A purity vow is a promise you make to God and your future husband. This is a promise that you are making to stay pure until after marriage. What steps will you take to maintain your purity? What will you refrain from doing?

_____

_____

_____

_____

_____

_____

_____

_____

_____

_____

_____

_____

_____

_____

_____

_____

_____

_____

_____

_____

_____

A Letter to My Husband

You will give this letter to your husband on your wedding day. What will you write to your husband? What would you like him to know about your journey?

_____
_____
_____
_____
_____
_____
_____
_____
_____
_____
_____
_____
_____
_____
_____
_____
_____
_____
_____
_____
_____
_____
_____

Bible Study Learn and Grow

Genesis 2–4: Adam and Eve
Genesis 15–17: Abram and Sarai
Genesis 29: Jacob and Rachel
Genesis 2:21–24 (NIV)
Ruth 1–4: Ruth and Boaz
Ezekiel 16:26
Ezekiel 23:1–49 (NLT)
1 Thessalonians 4:1–12 (NLT)
1 Corinthians 6:9–10
2 Timothy 2:22
1 Corinthians 7:2
2 Corinthians 12:21
2 Corinthians 6:14–18
Ephesians 5:3–5
Colossians 3:5
Psalms 101
Romans 12:1–2 (NIV)
1 Timothy 4:12 (NIV)
1 Corinthians 6:18 (NIV)
1 Corinthians 6:16–20 (MSG)
Titus 2:12 (NIV)
Colossians 3:5–8 (MSG)
Song of Solomon 6:8–9 (MSG)
Matthew 26:41

Works Cited

1. YouVersion. [Edmond, OK]: Life. Church, 2014.Bible. com/app. 10 June. 2014, 2015, and 2016. Versions: NIV, MSG, and KJV.
2. Norman Vincent Peale. Brainy Quotes. 2001–2014 Web. 10 June. 2014 www.brainyquote.com/quotes/quotes/n/normanvinc 130593.htm
3. CTI Reviews and Williams, K. Brian. Just the FACTS101: Marriages, Families, and Intimate Relationships. 3rd Edition. Content Technologies, Inc., 2012
4. Shannon L. Alder Quotable Quotes. Good Reads. 2015 Goodreads Inc. October 2015 http://www.goodreads. com/quotes/6565613-i-don-t-live-by-other-people-s-time-tables-i-live
5. Fernanda Miramontes-Landeros. Quote Garden 2015 Feb 2015. Web. September 2015. http://www. quotegarden.com/wise-words.html
6. Edmond Mbiaka. Quotes About Positive Inner Self. Good Reads. 2015 Goodreads Inc. Web October 2015. https://www.goodreads.com/quotes/tag/positive-inner-self
7. Roger Crawford. Good Reads. 2015 Goodreads Inc. Web October 2015. https://www.goodreads.com/quotes/ 496796-being-challenged-in-life-is-inevitable-being-defeated-is-optional

8. Deal Breaker. 2015 Oxford University Press. Web February 2015. http://www.oxforddictionaries.com/ us/definition/american_english/deal-breaker

9. Thomas S. Monson. Brainy Quotes. 2001–2015 BrainyQuote. Web February 2015.

10. Fornication. 2015 Merriam-Webster Dictionary. Web October 2015. http://www.merriam-webster.com/ dictionary/fornication

11. Temptation. 2015 Merriam-Webster Dictionary. Web October 2015. http://www.merriam-webster.com/ dictionary/temptation

12. Ezra Taft Benson. Good Reads. 2015 Goodreads Inc. Web October 2015. http://www.goodreads.com/ quotes/363779-when-we-put-god-first-all-other-things-fall-into

13. *My Big Fat Greek Wedding.* IMDb October 2015. 1990-2015 IMDb.com, Inc. An Amazon.com company. http://www.imdb.com/title/tt0259446/quotes

14. Rib Cage - Medical Art Library. Medical Art Library. 2017 Medical Art Library. www.medicalartlibrary. com/ribcage/

15. Audrey Hepburn. Brainy Quotes. 2001–2015 BrainyQuote. Web October 2015. http://www.brainy quote.com/quotes/keywords/woman.html#dRrr 01ftl7hJpmjC.99

16. Good. Dictionary.com Unabridged. Random House, Inc. October. 2016. <Dictionary.com http://www. dictionary.com/browse/good>.

17. Favor. Dictionary.com Unabridged. Random House, Inc. October. 2016. <Dictionary.com http://www. dictionary.com/browse/favor>.

18. Rachel McAdams. Brainy Quotes. 2001–2015 BrainyQuote. Web October 2015. http://www.brainy quote.com/quotes/keywords/fairytale.html#Jklk R2mw6PPcHMYq.99

19. Rabindranath Tagore. Brainy Quotes. 2001 - 2015 BrainyQuote. Web October 2015. http://www.brainy quote.com/quotes/keywords/envy.html#2uaiBgW2 vv9YkixM.99

20. Compare. 2016 Oxford University Press. https:// en.oxforddictionaries.com/definition/compare

21. Ian McShane. Brainy Quotes. 2001–2015 Web. October. 2015. http://www.brainyquote.com/quotes/ quotes/i/ianmcshane491447.html

22. Dr. Seuss. Quotable Quotes, Good Reads. 2015 Goodreads Inc. November 2015.
http://www.goodreads.com/quotes/7901-you-know-you-re-in-love-when-you-can-t-fall-asleep

23. Osayi Osar-Emokpae, Because You Deserve Love. Quotable Quotes, Good Reads. 2015 Goodreads Inc. December 2015.
http://www.goodreads.com/quotes/1010037-hold-on-to-the-thought-that-no-emotion-lasts-forever

24. Maya Angelou Quotable Quotes, Good Reads. 2015 Goodreads Inc. January 2015.
http://www.goodreads.com/quotes/225830-have-enough-courage-to-trust-love-one-more-time-and

25. T. D. Jakes, Quotable Quotes, Good Reads. 2015 Goodreads Inc. January 2015.
http://www.goodreads.com/quotes/105615-no-woman-wants-to-be-in-submission-to-a-man

26. Eric Ludy. AZQuotes.com. Wind and Fly LTD, 2016. February 2016. http://www.azquotes.com/quote/ 1116408

27. Benjamin Disraeli. QuotationsPage.com and Michael Moncur. October 2016. http://www.quotationspage. com/quote/23684.html

28. "What Does a Land Surveyor Do?" The Courthouse Direct.com. 19 December 2016. Bloghttp://info.court housedirect.com/blog/bid/217136/What-Does-a-Land-Surveyor-Do

Printed in the United States
By Bookmasters